D1105207

Sports Illustrated KIDS

STARS OF SPORTS

ALY RAISMAN

GOLD-MEDAL GYMNAST

by Matt Chandler

CAPSTONE PRESS
a capstone imprint

Stars of Sports is published by Capstone Press, an imprint of Capstone.
1710 Roe Crest Drive, North Mankato, Minnesota 56003
www.capstonepub.com

**Library of Congress Cataloging-in-Publication Data is available on the Library
of Congress website.**
ISBN: 978-1-4966-8385-4 (hardcover)
ISBN: 978-1-4966-8436-3 (eBook PDF)

Summary: Aly Raisman started gymnastics when she was just 2 years old. In 2011,
she helped the U.S. gymnastics team win the World Championships. The next
year she participated in her first Olympic Games in London. Discover more about
Raisman's gymnastics career highlights.

Editorial Credits
Editor: Anna Butzer; Designer: Sarah Bennett; Media Researcher: Eric Gohl;
Production Specialist: Laura Manthe

Image Credits
AP Photo: Koji Sasahara, 8; Getty Images: Boston Globe, 12, 21, Ronald Martinez,
11, SOPA Images, 28, Stringer/Darren McCollester, 7, 20; Newscom: Reuters/Dylan
Martinez, 10, ZUMA Press/Daniel DeSlover, 6, ZUMA Press/Erich Schlegel, 23;
Shutterstock: Alex Kravtsov, 1, DFree, 27, Leonard Zhukovsky, cover, Petr Toman,
25; Sports Illustrated: Al Tielemans, 19, Erick W. Rasco, 9, John Biever, 5, 16, Peter
Read Miller, 14, 15

Direct Quotations
Page 8, "When we saw her . . ." Just Gymnastics, "Aly Raisman: Quest for Gold,"
May 15, 2013, 1:10:59, https://www.youtube.com/watch?v=qjVqzPQ5lfo
Accessed on March 20, 2020

Page 12, "There's no time for . . ." livegymnastics15, "Aly Raisman Story," November
9, 2011, 5:01, https://www.youtube.com/watch?v=9rk0a6UjZRQ
Accessed on March 16, 2020

Page 13, "At the end of . . ." #Overshare, "Prepping for Rio 2016, Aly Raisman
Reflects on Her Gymnastics Career and DWTS," November 18, 2013, 7:56,
https://www.youtube.com/watch?v=JeHA_yEWhBU
Accessed on March 16, 2020

Page 18, "one of the best . . ." USA Gymnastics, "Raisman Returns!," December 1,
2014, 8:07, https://www.youtube.com/watch?v=8jAO8vivdLc
Accessed on March 16, 2020

All internet sites appearing in back matter were available and accurate when this
book was sent to press.

Printed in the United States of America.
PA117

TABLE OF CONTENTS

Glossary terms are **BOLD** on first use.

GOLDEN MOMENT

Aly Raisman stood in the corner of the mat. Her body was frozen in place like a statue. She was about to perform the biggest **floor exercise** routine of her career. It was 2012, and Raisman was in London, England, for the Summer Olympics. She was part of the U.S. Women's Gymnastics team known as the "Fierce Five." Together they would leave London with a gold medal for the team competition. Here, Raisman was on her own. She took a deep breath. It was time.

The music began and Raisman sprinted across the floor. She launched herself into the air and executed a perfect series of tumbling flips. Resetting, she continued to dazzle the fans and the judges with her routine. When she landed her final flip, the crowd erupted. Raisman ran into the arms of her teammates. She had won the gold!

FACT

Raisman became the first American woman in Olympic history to win the gold medal for the floor exercise.

CHAPTER ONE

GROWING UP A GYMNAST

Like many Olympians, Aly was born to parents who were athletes. Her mom, Lynn, was a gymnast, and her dad, Rick, was a hockey player. She was the oldest of the Raismans' four children. Growing up in Needham, Massachusetts, Aly began taking gymnastics classes when she was only 2 years old.

>>> Aly, her dad, Rick, and her brother, Brett

>>> Aly and her mom, Lynn

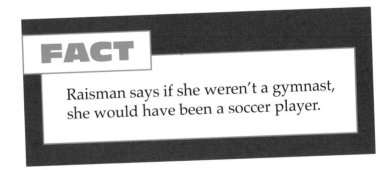

FACT

Raisman says if she weren't a gymnast, she would have been a soccer player.

By the time she was 10, Aly was telling her mom she was going to be an Olympic gymnast. Aly's parents enrolled her in an **elite** gymnastics school in Burlington, Massachusetts. Mihai and Sylvie Brestyan coached Aly at their gymnastics club. Under their guidance, she would soon become an elite gymnast.

THE SPARK

As a 10-year-old, Aly wasn't your typical gymnast, and Mihai Brestyan knew it. "When we saw her, right away she had this sparkle," he said. "Aly, from the beginning, looked like a very determined kid. She knew she wanted to be famous."

Raisman credits Mihai Brestyan with helping her take that ability to the next level. He was a demanding coach. She had to be at the gym every day. Missing a day was rarely an option. Raisman's senior prom was two months before the 2012 Olympics. Her coaches gave her one night off to go. Then it was back to the gym.

>>> Mihai Brestyan and Raisman

>>> Raisman has said that the encouragement from her coach, Mihai Brestyan, kept her motivated during the most difficult times of her training.

By high school, Raisman was a rising star in gymnastics. Her prediction of competing in the Olympics looked like it might come true in 2009.

She had qualified to compete at the 2009 Junior Pan Am Games in Aracaju, Brazil. Raisman and her teammates dominated the games. They captured the team gold medal. Raisman won the individual gold for vault and floor exercise.

〉〉〉 Raisman and fellow gymnast Alicia Sacramone

One of Raisman's teammates was 2008 Olympian Alicia Sacramone. Raisman credits her with being a mentor and a role model. Could Raisman follow in Sacramone's footsteps? Her family, friends, and coaches thought she could. And for Raisman, it was the ultimate goal.

FINDING BALANCE

While her friends were going to the mall and hanging out, Raisman was training. Normal teen activities, such as dating, weren't an option.

"There's no time for a boyfriend," she said during her senior year at Needham High School. "After I'm done with gymnastics I can have time, but I'm basically here (at the gym) all the time."

〉〉〉 Raisman training at her coach's gym in Massachusetts

Her parents helped her find some balance between gymnastics and being a normal teenager. She stayed in public school through her junior year. She would compete around the country. Raisman traveled to Texas, Florida, and California. She competed internationally in Brazil, Italy, and Australia. Each time, she returned home to school and to her friends.

"At the end of the day you realize if you don't have your family and friends to go home to, it doesn't mean anything," Raisman said.

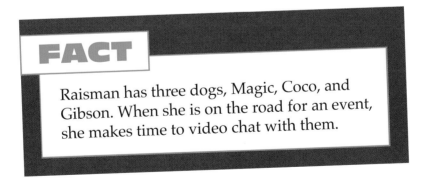

FACT

Raisman has three dogs, Magic, Coco, and Gibson. When she is on the road for an event, she makes time to video chat with them.

At 10 years old, Raisman told her mom she would be an Olympic gymnast. At 18, that dream became a reality. Raisman earned a spot on the 2012 U.S. Women's Olympic team to compete at the Summer Games in London. The hard work and sacrifice had paid off. Raisman had already won more than a dozen medals in international competition. Now it was time to add an Olympic medal to her collection.

》》》 Raisman competing in floor exercise

For her individual events, Raisman's best chance to medal was on the floor exercise. She has always said the bars are her least favorite event. Though she performed well on the balance beam, it wasn't her strongest event. If Raisman was going to capture an individual gold medal, it would likely be for her floor routine. Standing between Raisman and the gold medal was a group of the best gymnasts in the world.

BALANCING FOR BRONZE

Competing in the finals of the balance beam, Raisman was behind. She wasn't expected to win a medal in the event. Russian gymnast Victoria Komova took to the beam right before Raisman. The medal favorite fell from the beam during her routine. That gave Raisman a chance. A great routine could earn her a surprise medal.

Raisman delivered. She completed her routine with a **Double Arabian** dismount. The crowd cheered. Would it be enough? She waited nervously with her coach and teammates for the score to be announced. She needed a score of 15.066 to capture the bronze medal. The judges ruled, and it was devastating for Raisman. Her score of 14.966 left her in fourth place. At least for a moment. Her coach quickly challenged the score, and it was reviewed. The judges raised Raisman's score to 15.066. She won the bronze!

⟨⟨⟨ Raisman leaps onto the beam to start her routine at the 2012 Olympics.

TEAM GOLD

Raisman had earned her gold in floor and a surprising bronze in the beam. But being part of the Olympic team was a dream. The 2012 Women's Team, called the Fierce Five, consisted of Raisman, Gabby Douglas, McKayla Maroney, Kyla Ross, and Jordyn Wieber in London.

All of the athletes were between 15 and 18 years old. The teens lived together in the Olympic Village. They ate together and trained together. When Raisman was competing in an individual event, her teammates were there. They cheered each other on to victory. And together, they captured the team gold. Raisman called the night of the team finals "one of the best nights of my life . . . exactly what you dream of."

The Fierce Five took the world by storm. The girls were featured on magazine covers. They filmed commercials. They appeared on the late-night talk shows. They were true celebrities!

 The Fierce Five from left to right: McKayla Maroney, Kyla Ross, Aly Raisman, Gabrielle Douglas, and Jordyn Wieber

FACT

Raisman says she wears as many as 15 tight hair ties to keep her hair in place when she trains.

CHAPTER FOUR

RETURN TO THE OLYMPICS

After winning three medals in the 2012 Games, Raisman needed a break. The nonstop training and pressure had taken a toll. She stopped training and enjoyed life as a new celebrity. She went to the beach. She spent time with her family and friends. Even though she stepped away, Raisman always planned to return to the Olympics in 2016.

〉〉〉 Raisman signs autographs during an event in 2014.

<<< Raisman trains with her coach at Brestyan's Gym.

Though she was a **veteran**, Raisman faced a different type of pressure. As a three-time Olympic medalist, all eyes would be on her. She also faced long odds. It is rare for a gymnast to compete in more than one Olympics. Greats including Mary Lou Retton, Nastia Liukin, Shawn Johnson, McKayla Maroney, and Alicia Sacramone only made one Olympic team. In a sport dominated by athletes with ages ranging from 16 to 18, Raisman would be 22 if she made it to Rio.

OVERCOMING THE ODDS

In December 2015 Raisman was training with the national team. During warm-ups for the floor exercise, she felt a sharp pain in her left ankle. Tests would show she had a partial tear in her **ligament**. Doctors put her in a special boot. She was in danger of missing the Rio Olympics.

Raisman has always been very confident in her ability. Her ankle injury changed that. She worried that the younger gymnasts coming up were better than her. She feared the injury might end her plan to return to the Olympics.

Training to Be the Best

Training for the Olympics is a full-time job. When Raisman is in training, she hits the gym by 8:30 a.m. Most days she doesn't return home until 9 p.m. Her days are filled with challenging workouts. She climbs ropes using only her arms. She runs. She builds strength on the bars. She practices each routine over and over. Each step must be perfect. Each landing must be flawless. That dedication has paid off with six Olympic medals!

>>> Raisman training in 2015

Instead of giving up, Raisman got back in the gym. She trained two hours each day in her walking boot. She couldn't do her routines, but she worked to keep her strength and **agility** up.

By January, Raisman was cleared to resume full training. Soon she was back to form and ready to return to the Olympics!

THE FINAL FIVE

The 2016 U.S. Women's Gymnastics team would be the last to feature five competitors. The **International Olympic Committee** (IOC) announced it was reducing the teams to four athletes for the Tokyo Games in 2020. Raisman and her 2016 teammates, nicknamed the "Final Five," wanted to leave a **legacy**.

On the individual side, Raisman had more to accomplish. Before the games were over she would double her Olympic medal total to six. In addition to the team gold medal, Raisman added a silver medal in the **All-Around**. When it came time to defend her gold in the floor exercise, Raisman delivered a dynamic performance. She earned a 15.43 score that put her in first place, and on track for another gold.

Teammate Simone Biles followed Raisman's performance with a near flawless routine. As Biles watched her 15.93 score post, the first to embrace her was Raisman. Biles had taken the gold. Instead of being sad, Raisman celebrated with her teammate.

Leader of the Pack

Her Olympic teammates in Rio had a nickname for Raisman—Grandma. At 22, Raisman was the oldest of the American gymnasts on the 2016 squad. She earned a reputation for taking naps and going to bed early. While the teens were up having fun, "Grandma" was resting. Her veteran leadership was an important part of the team's gold medal success in Rio. Teammate Simone Biles called Raisman by her nickname. She also called her a leader and role model for the younger gymnasts.

CHAPTER FIVE
LIFE AFTER RIO

Raisman stood on the podium in Rio in 2016 and collected her sixth Olympic medal. There were rumors that she would try and return to the 2020 Olympics in Tokyo. However, she confirmed she was not training for the Olympics, or any other competition. Instead, for the first time, she is relaxing. She is spending time with friends and family. She is not worried about the next competition or the next double training session. Raisman spent many years of her life in elite level gymnastics. Today, she is happy just being a "regular" woman.

Raisman at the 2018 People's Choice Awards 〉〉〉

INSPIRING THE WORLD

Though she hasn't been competing or training, she has been busy. The gold medalist is an author, a model, and has appeared on television countless times. She is a popular speaker on college campuses across the U.S. She hopes to use her fame and success to inspire young athletes. With six gold medals, Aly Raisman will definitely be an **inspiration** to future generations of gymnasts.

TIMELINE

1994 Alexandra Rose Raisman was born in Needham, Massachusetts, on May 25

1996 Takes her first ever gymnastics class when just 2 years old

2010 Wins her first gold medal, competing at the Pacific Rim

2011 Captures gold at the World Championships in Tokyo

2012 Graduates from high school while training for her first Olympics

2012 Wins two gold medals at her first Olympics

2013 Appears on the reality television show *Dancing with the Stars*

2016 Returns to the Olympics and wins three more medals

2018 Becomes a *New York Times* Bestselling author when her biography, *Fierce*, is published that same year

2019 Appears in her first film, *Charlie's Angels*

GLOSSARY

AGILITY (uh-GI-luh-tee)—the ability to move fast and easily

ALL-AROUND (all-uh-ROUND)—the all-around champion earns the highest total score from all four gymnastic events

DOUBLE ARABIAN (DUH-buhl uh-RAY-bee-uhn)—a somersault beginning with a backward entry into a half twist, followed by two consecutive front flips

ELITE (i-LEET)—among the best

FLOOR EXERCISE (FLOR EK-suhr-syz)—gymnastics event in which movements are performed in a routine on the floor

INSPIRATION (in-spihr-AY-shun)—something that fills someone with an emotion, an idea, or an attitude

INTERNATIONAL OLYMPIC COMMITTEE (in-tur-NASH-uh-nuhl oh-LIM-pik kuh-MI-tee)—a non-governmental sports organization that is responsible for organizing the Summer and Winter Olympic Games

LEGACY (LEG-uh-see)—qualities and actions that one is remembered for; something that is passed on to future generations

LIGAMENT (LIG-uh-muhnt)—a band of tissue that connects bones to bones

VETERAN (VET-ur-uhn)—someone with a lot of experience in a profession, a position, or an activity

READ MORE

Chandler, Matt. *Gymnastics: A Guide for Athletes and Fans.* North Mankato, MN: Capstone Press, 2020.

Gitlin, Marty. *Olympic Gymnastics Legends.* Mankato, MN: Black Rabbit Books, 2021.

Leigh, Anna. *Aly Raisman: Athlete and Activist.* Minneapolis: Lerner Publications, 2019.

INTERNET SITES

Artistic Gymnastics
www.olympic.org/gymnastics-artistic

International Gymnastics Hall of Fame
www.ighof.com/

USA Gymnastics
usagym.org/pages/women/pages/index.html

INDEX